Woods
Irons,
and
Greens

Contents

Tiger Woods 2

Rules and Plays 8

Design a Golf Course . . . 16

Beat Tiger Woods
in the Masters 24

Tiger Woods

Written by Dean Iversen
Illustrated by Nicolas van Pallandt

Eldrick Tiger Woods is a great golfer.
In 1996, he was named Sportsman of the Year
by *Sports Illustrated* magazine.
You can buy lots of books about him.
You can buy lots of videos about him.
You can find out about him on the Internet.
You can read about him in the newspaper.

It has not been easy for Tiger Woods
to become a good golfer.
It has taken a lot of time and effort.
He has had to work hard at his golf.

Two very special people have helped Tiger.
These special people are his mother and father.
They taught him how to play golf.
They taught him how to be a kind, caring person.
They taught him that you can always learn new things.
You can learn things when you are playing well,
and you can learn things when you are not playing well.

What sorts of things did Tiger's parents teach him?

3

When Tiger was a little boy, he would sit in his highchair
and look at all the things around him.
He saw his father hitting hundreds of golf balls into a net.
As soon as he could walk, Tiger wanted to hit a golf ball, too.
When he was three, he won his first golf contest.
The other children in the tournament were older than Tiger.
When he was four, Tiger made his first *birdie*.
A *birdie* is when you get the ball into the hole
in one hit less than *par*.
Par is the number of hits it should take a good golfer
to get the ball in the hole.
Each day, Tiger would hit hundreds of golf balls into the net,
just the same as his father had.

Tiger's father knew Tiger could be a really good golfer.
He knew Tiger could be the best in the world.
He knew Tiger needed to learn how to play
without letting people and noise throw him off his game.
Each time Tiger went to hit the ball,
his father would try to throw him off.
His father would talk and yell and do silly things.
Tiger learned not to be thrown off his game.

Tiger also had a great role model.
His role model was a golfer named Jack Nicklaus.
Tiger wanted to be better
than Jack Nicklaus.
When Tiger was little,
he was on a television show.
On the television show, he said
that one day he would beat Jack Nicklaus.

What is a role model? Do you have one?

4

Tiger made a chart.
He put all the big golf tournaments on it.
On the chart, Tiger also put
how old Jack Nicklaus was when he won each tournament.
Tiger left a gap to put how old he will have been
when he won the tournaments.

Tiger filled in the first gap on his chart in 1997.
That year, he was the youngest player
to win the Masters Tournament.
As the ball fell into the last hole,
Tiger punched his hand into the air.
Then he hugged his mother and his father.
He said, "I think every time I hug my Mom and Pop
after a tournament, it's over.
I accomplished my goal,
and to share it with them is something special."
President Bill Clinton said the greatest shot of the tournament
was Tiger hugging his parents.

RULES AND PLAYS

Written by
Mark Iversen

Illustrated by
Fraser Williamson

To play a round of golf you need these things:

- Golf clubs.
  You may have a set of your own
  or you can rent them at the golf course.
  A set is most often made up of 14 clubs.
  There are many kinds of golf clubs.
  There are woods, and irons,
  and putters, and wedges.

- A golf bag.
  In some places,
  people carry their clubs on a spike.
  The spike can only carry a few clubs.
  You can push the bottom
  of the spike into the ground
  while you hit the ball.

What do
you need before
you can start
your game of
golf?

8

- Some golf balls.
  You will need more than one golf ball
  because you often lose balls when you play.

- Some golf tees.
  You put your golf ball on the golf tee
  at the start of each hole.
  The golf tee holds the ball up off the ground
  so you can hit it.

- A score card.
  You will get a score card
  at the golf course.
  At the end of each hole,
  write down how many times
  you hit the ball
  before it went into the hole.
  At the end of the game,
  add up all the numbers.

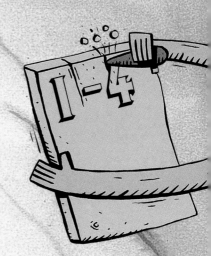

- Some other people to play with.
  You can play by yourself if you like.
  It is more fun if you have other people to play with.

When you have all these things,
you can start your game of golf.

The starting place for each hole
is the part of the golf course called the tee.
At each tee, there will be two markers.
The markers show you where to hit the ball from.
You can hit the ball from anywhere behind the markers.
This area is called the tee
because this is where you sit your ball on the tee.
You are trying to hit your ball from the tee into the hole.

Each time you hit the ball, it is called a stroke.
When you get the ball into the hole,
you add up how many strokes it took you.
Then you write the number of strokes on your score card.

The hole is found on an area called the green.
Greens can be any shape.
They have very short grass so the ball rolls well.
The hole has a flag in it
so you can see where it is from far away.

Between the tee and the green
is the fairway.
A fairway is like a grass road.
You need to follow the fairway
to get to the hole.

Why do you think the grass needs to be short on the green?

After you have hit your tee shot,
it is the next person's turn.
When everyone has had their first shot,
the person whose ball is the farthest away from the hole
has the next shot.

Sometimes there are trees by the fairway.
Sometimes there are lakes in the fairway.
Sometimes you may lose your ball in the trees and lakes.
If you lose your ball, you can use another ball.
If you lose your ball,
you have to add 1 point to your score for that hole.

Your ball might land in a place where it is hard to hit.
It may be behind some long grass or in a little hole.
You can pick your ball up and move it.
You can only move it about 6 inches (15 cm).
You cannot move it closer to the hole.

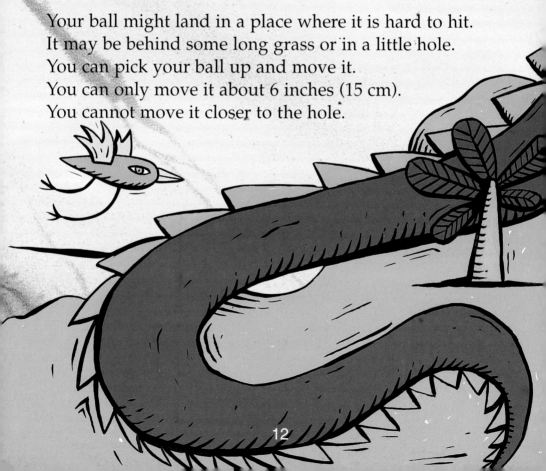

Your ball could also land in a bunker or sand trap.
A bunker is a large shallow hole.
It may have leaves or twigs in it.
You cannot move these leaves or twigs,
even if they are in the way.
Bunkers that are full of sand are called sand traps.

Each hole has a number of strokes that it should take
to get the ball from the tee into the hole.
This number is called par.
If it takes you more strokes,
it is called a bogey:
1 more stroke – bogey
2 more strokes – double bogey
3 more strokes – triple bogey
4 more strokes – quadruple bogey

If it takes you 1 stroke less than par,
it is called a birdie.
If it takes you 2 strokes less than par,
it is called an eagle.
If it takes you 3 strokes less than par,
it is called an albatross.
If you get the ball
in the hole in one stroke,
it is called a hole in one.

When you get to the end of the 18 holes,
add up your scores for each of the holes.
This is your final score.

Now you know how to play a round of golf.
Happy golfing!

Design a Golf Course

Written by Mark Iversen

It is great fun to sit and draw
a golf course.
You could make a model of it,
or you could even
make a golf course on a computer.
Before you start
to make your golf course,
there are many things
to think about.
Here are some things
that will help you to make
the best course in the world.

You might want your golf course to be the course at Augusta where Tiger Woods won the Masters. That is the course that Greg Norman says is the hardest but the most fun to play on.

What do you need for your golf course?

You will need 18 holes.
Each golf hole needs

- ## A tee ground.
  That is the place
  where you begin each hole.
  Two markers show the golfers
  where to hit the ball from.

- ## A fairway.
  Make the grass on the fairway nice and short.

- ## A green.
  Put the hole in the putting green.
  Put a flag in the hole.
  Make the grass on the green very short.
  Make sure there are no bumps on your green.

You also need a clubhouse.
This is where the golfers go after the game.
The tee for the first hole
should be near the clubhouse.

Think about where your golf course is.
If it is in a town,
you will need buildings and roads near by.
If it is in the country, you will need to put in
trees and fields and maybe hills.

When you have made the big picture,
look at your golf course again.

You do not want all the 18 holes to be the same.

You can make the holes any length.
Make your holes between 250 yards (229 m)
and 600 yards (548 m) long.
Each hole has a par.
A par is the number of hits
that it would take a good golfer
to get from the tee into the hole.
Here are some pars:
- par 3: 250 yards (229 m)
- par 4: 251–470 yards (230–430 m)
- par 5: at least 471 yards (431 m)

Add some trees.

Add the trees along the side of the fairway.
This will make it hard for a golfer to take short cuts.
Don't put the trees in the middle of the fairway.

Add some water.

You may like to make your golf course near the sea.
This will make it look nice.
It will also make the course harder.
The wind coming off the sea makes it hard
for some golfers to hit the ball in the right place.
Add some lakes that the golfers
have to hit the ball over.

Augusta golf course, where the Masters is played, has a large lake that the golfers have to hit the ball across.

Add some sand traps.

Sand traps are big holes, filled with sand.

Add some roughs.

Roughs on golf courses
are where the grass has not been cut short.
They are along the side of the fairways, by the trees.

Make a hole a funny shape.

Make some holes you can see from the tee.
Make them straight.
Make other holes that go around corners.
These holes are called doglegs.

Make the greens.

Make them any size or shape.
Make the holes in the green.

Add the clubhouse.

Make the clubhouse big enough for lots of golfers to come into after they have played a round of golf. Lots of clubhouses have big windows so people can sit and watch the other people playing.

What does your course look like?
Will all the best players
want to come and play on your course?

Beat Tiger Woods
in the Masters

Written by Dean Iversen
Illustrated by Nicolas van Pallandt

Play against Tiger Woods
in the last four holes of the Masters Golf Tournament.
Here is a game you can play on your own or with friends.

How to Play

You will need one dice, something to mark your place on the game board, a pen, and some paper.

1) Make a score card like the one on page 25.

2) Turn to pages 26–27.
    Place your markers on the tee for the 15th hole.

3) Read how Tiger played the hole.

4) Take turns throwing the dice.
    Move your marker the number on the dice.

5) Each time you throw the dice,
    put one point on your score card.

6) If you land in a bunker or in the crowd,
   throw the dice again.
   If it is a 1, 2, or 3, add one point to your score card.

7) When you get to the green, throw the dice.
   If it is a 1, 2, or 3, then it took you two putts
   to get the ball into the hole.
   Add two points to your score card.
   If it is a 4, 5, or 6, then it took you one putt
   to get the ball into the hole.
   Add one point to your score card.

8) At the end of each hole,
   add up the numbers on your score card.

9) After you have played the 18th hole,
   add up all the numbers on your score card.
   If your score is lower than Tiger's score, you win!

Name	15th	16th	17th	18th	Total
Tiger	ＨＨＴ	III	IIII	IIII	16

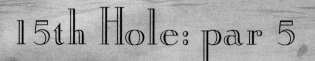

15th Hole: par 5

Tiger played a bad tee shot.
It landed on the 17th fairway.
His next shot landed to the right of the green.
It was in the crowd.
Tiger chipped the ball onto the green.
His first putt rolled past the hole.
His next putt went into the hole.
He scored a par.

When you have
played this game,
make up another
one.

15a

15b 15c 15d

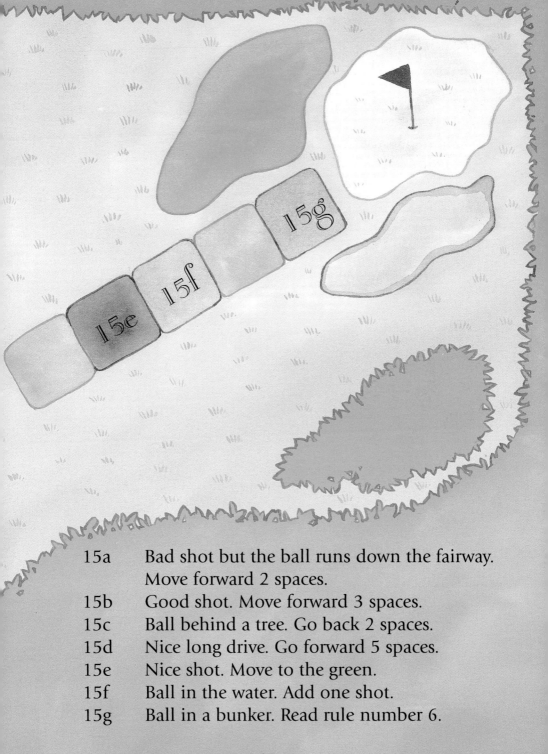

15a   Bad shot but the ball runs down the fairway. Move forward 2 spaces.

15b   Good shot. Move forward 3 spaces.

15c   Ball behind a tree. Go back 2 spaces.

15d   Nice long drive. Go forward 5 spaces.

15e   Nice shot. Move to the green.

15f   Ball in the water. Add one shot.

15g   Ball in a bunker. Read rule number 6.

16th Hole: par 3

Tiger landed his tee shot on the back of the green.
His first putt rolled past the hole.
His next putt went into the hole.
He scored a par.

16a   Wind helps your shot. Go to the green.
16b   Ball in the water. Add 1 shot.
16c   Ball in a bunker. Read rule number 6.

17th Hole: par 4

Tiger hit a long tee shot that landed on the fairway. His good tee shot made it easy for him to get par on this hole.

17a   Good shot. Move to the green.
17b   Ball in a good place. Move forward 2 spaces.
17c   Ball in the trees. Go back three spaces.
17d   Ball in a bunker. Read rule number 6.
17e   Hit over the top of the green. Go back 3 spaces.

18th Hole: par 4

Tiger hooked his tee shot off to the left of the fairway.
Tiger's next shot went past the hole.
It took him two putts to get the ball into the hole.
He scored a par.

18a

If you beat Tiger Woods, you could have the trophy on the title page.

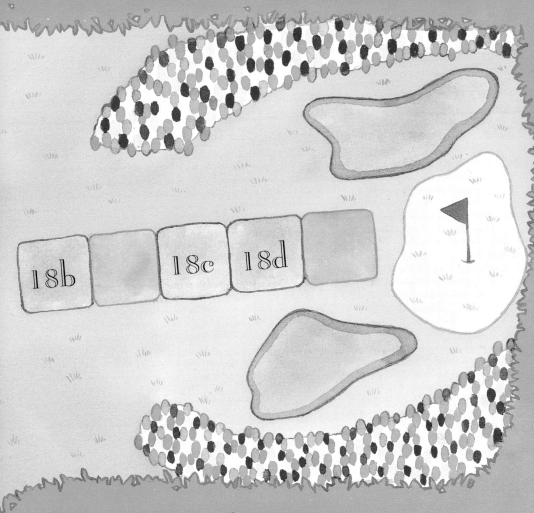

18a   Good shot. Go forward 2 spaces.
18b   Ball in the crowd. Read rule number 6.
18c   Ball in a bunker. Read rule number 6.
18d   Ball out of bounds. Add one shot.

Tiger's total score for the last four holes
was 16 shots.
What was your score?

Index

albatross   15
Augusta golf course   16, 21

Beat Tiger Woods game   24–31
birdie   4, 15
bogey   15
bunkers   14, 28, 29

clubhouse   18, 23

doglegs   22

eagle   15

fairway   11, 12, 18, 20, 22, 26, 27, 29, 30
flag   11, 18

golf bag   8
golf balls   4, 9,
golf clubs   8
golf course   10
     design   16–23
golf tees   9
golf tournaments   4, 6, 24

golfers   2, 4, 6, 18, 20, 23
green   10, 18, 22

hole   10–11, 12, 15, 18
hole in one   15
holes (18th)   15, 18, 20, 25, 30

Nicklaus, Jack   4, 6

par   4, 15, 20, 26, 28, 30

rough   22
rules and play   8–15

sand traps   14, 22
score card   9, 10, 24, 25
strokes   10, 15

tee   10, 18
trees along fairways   20

Woods, Tiger   2–7
     game   24–31
     parents   2, 4, 6
     role model   4